The Internal Portraits

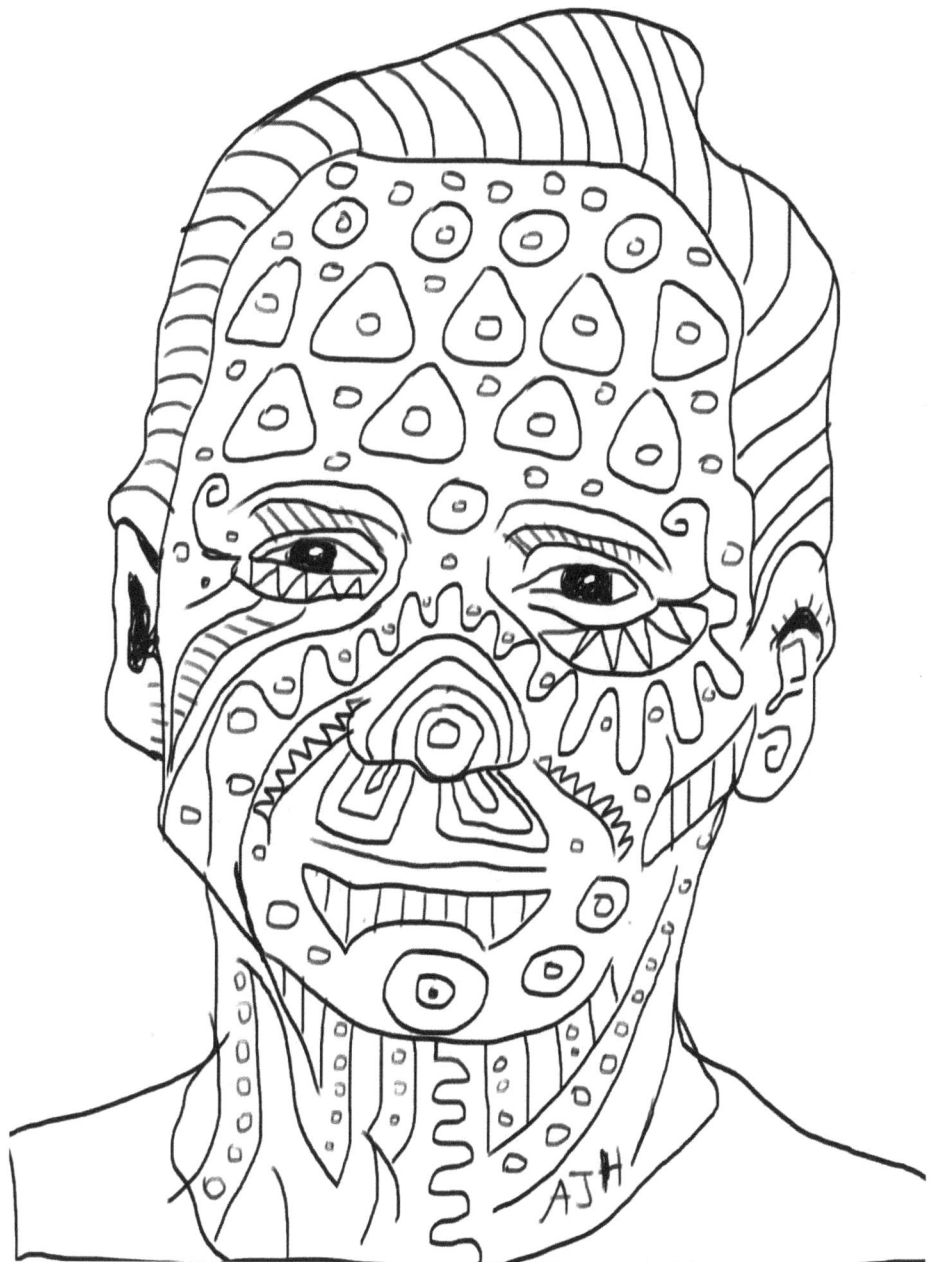

AJH

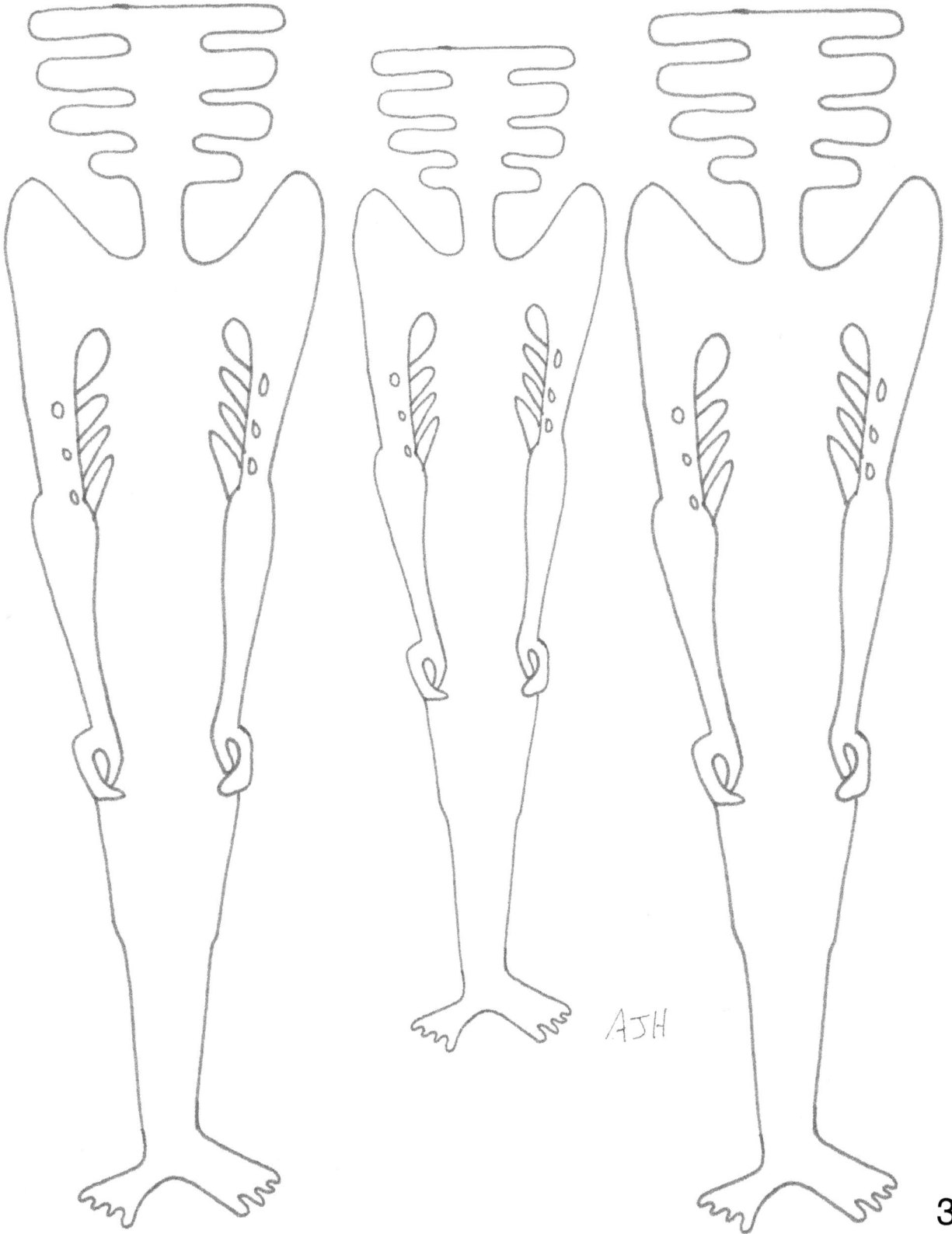

AJH

3

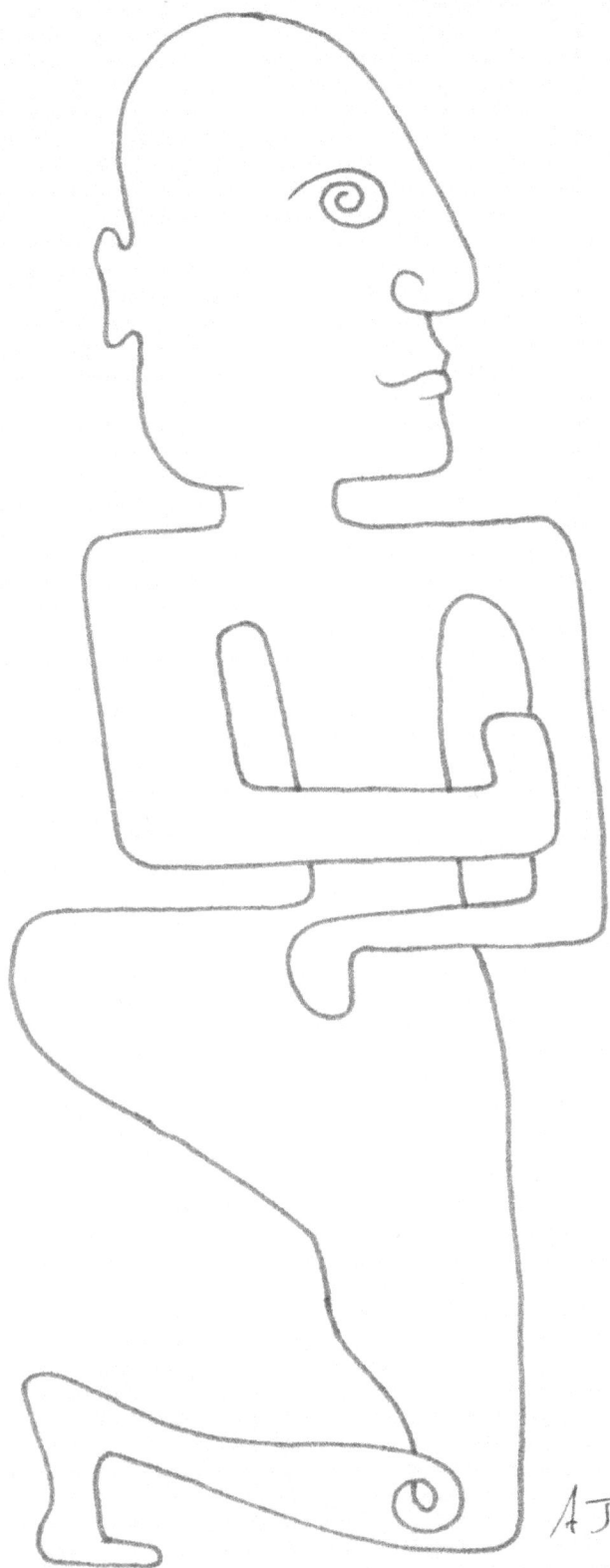

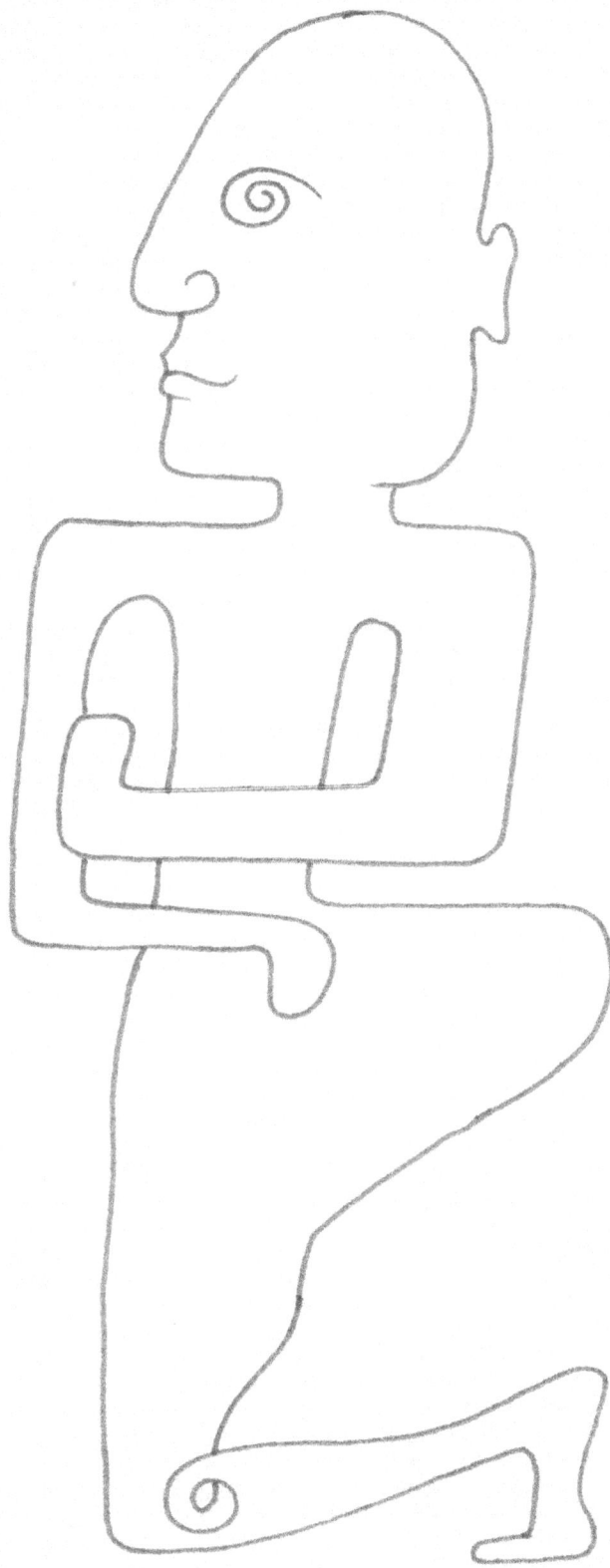

4

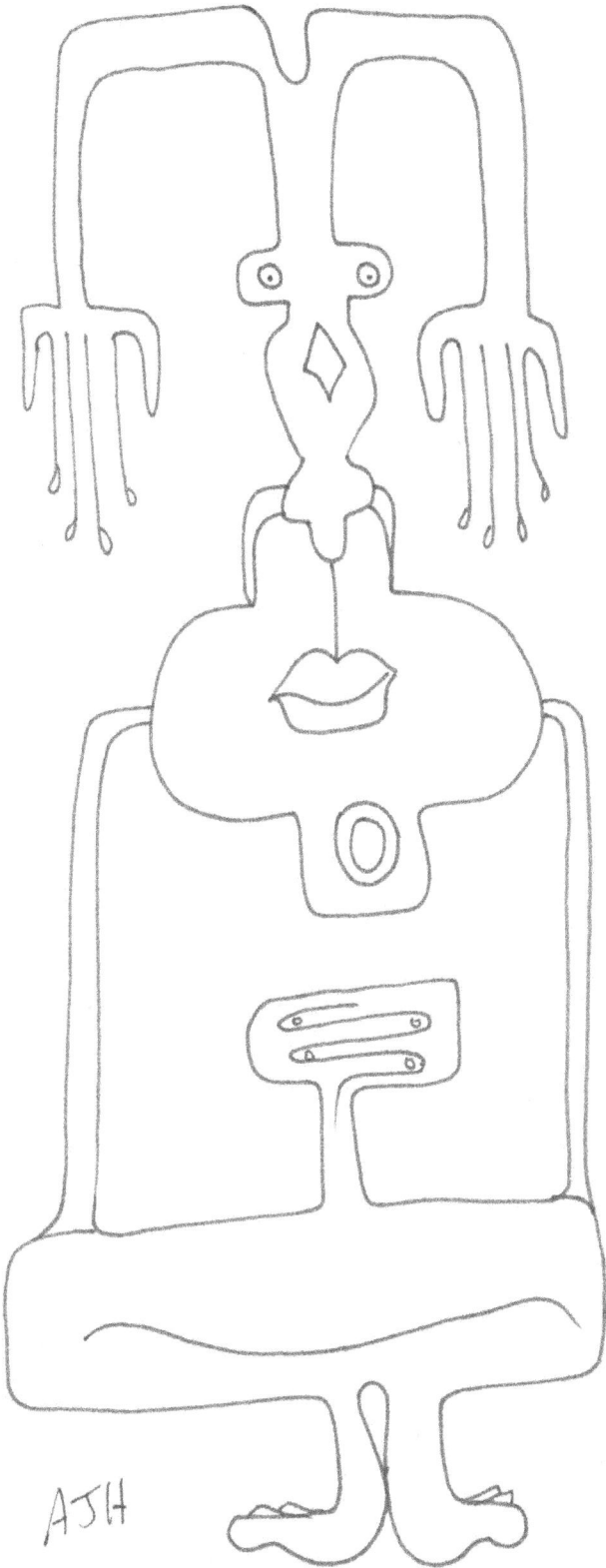

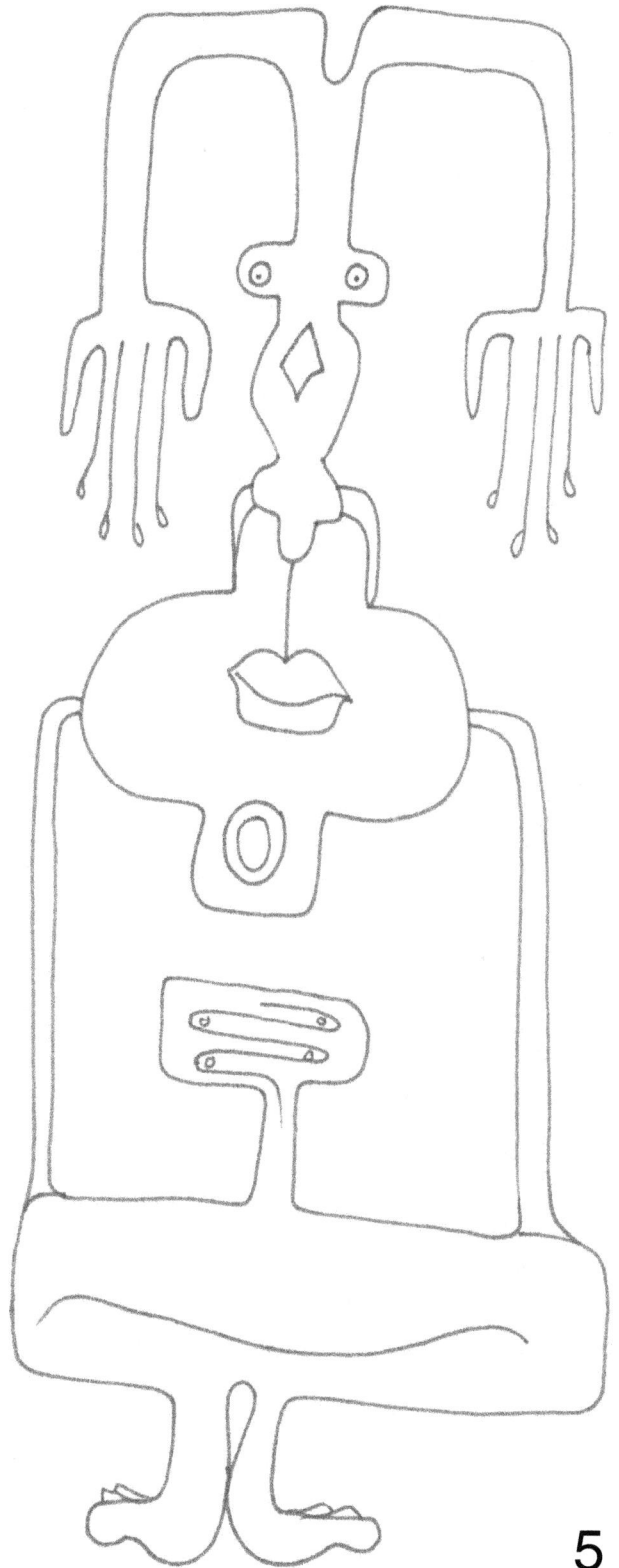

AJH

5

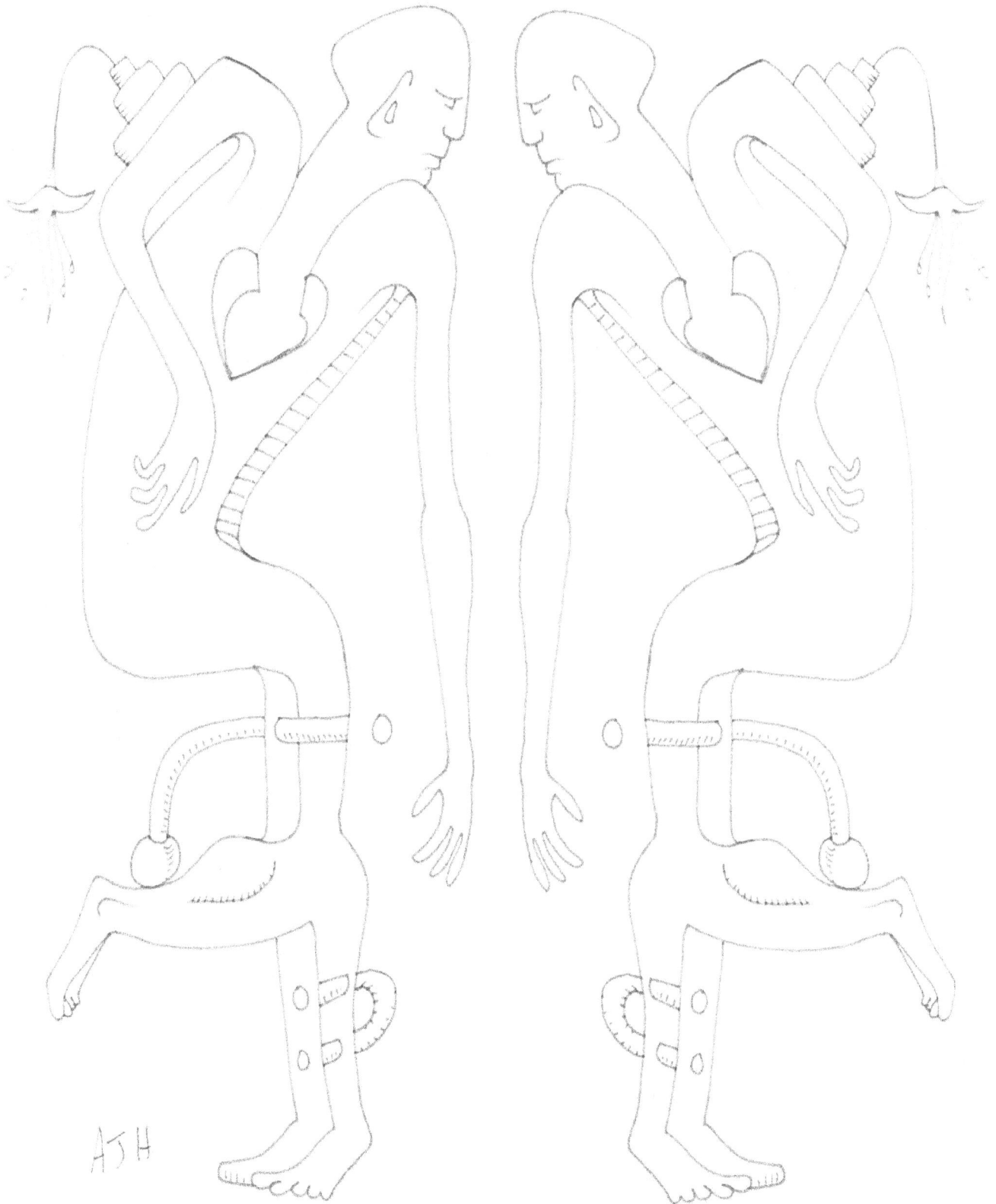

6

AJH

AJH

8

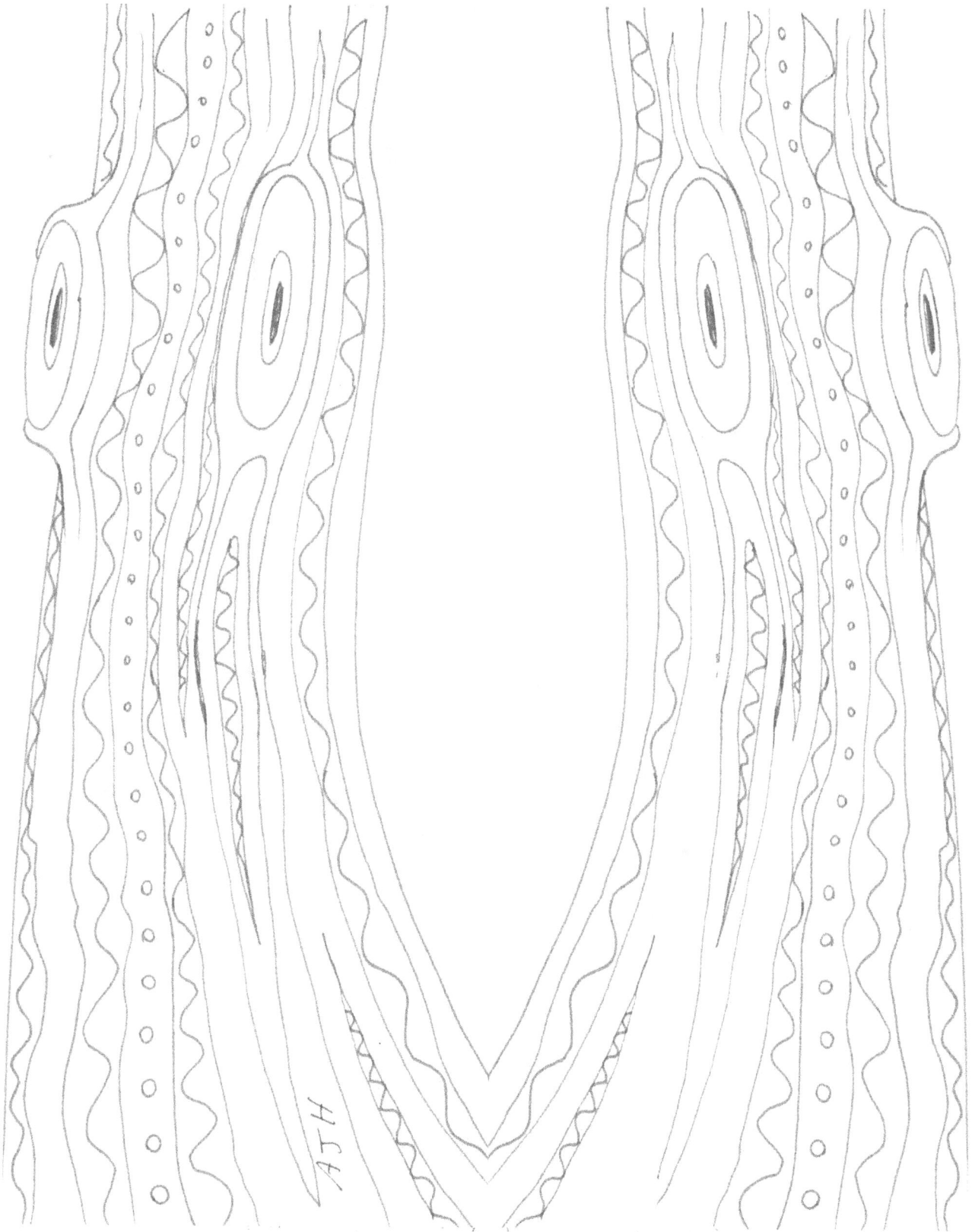

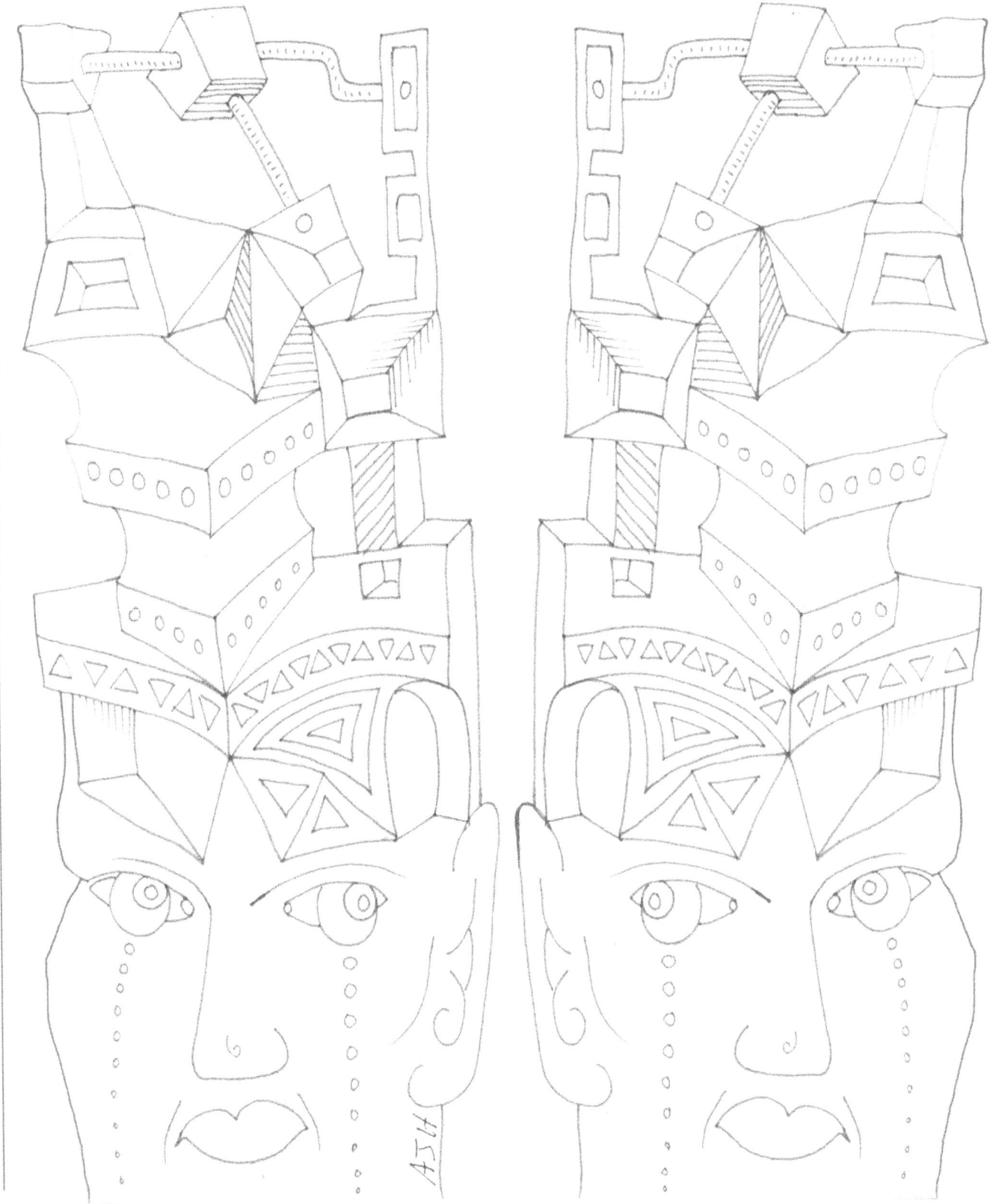

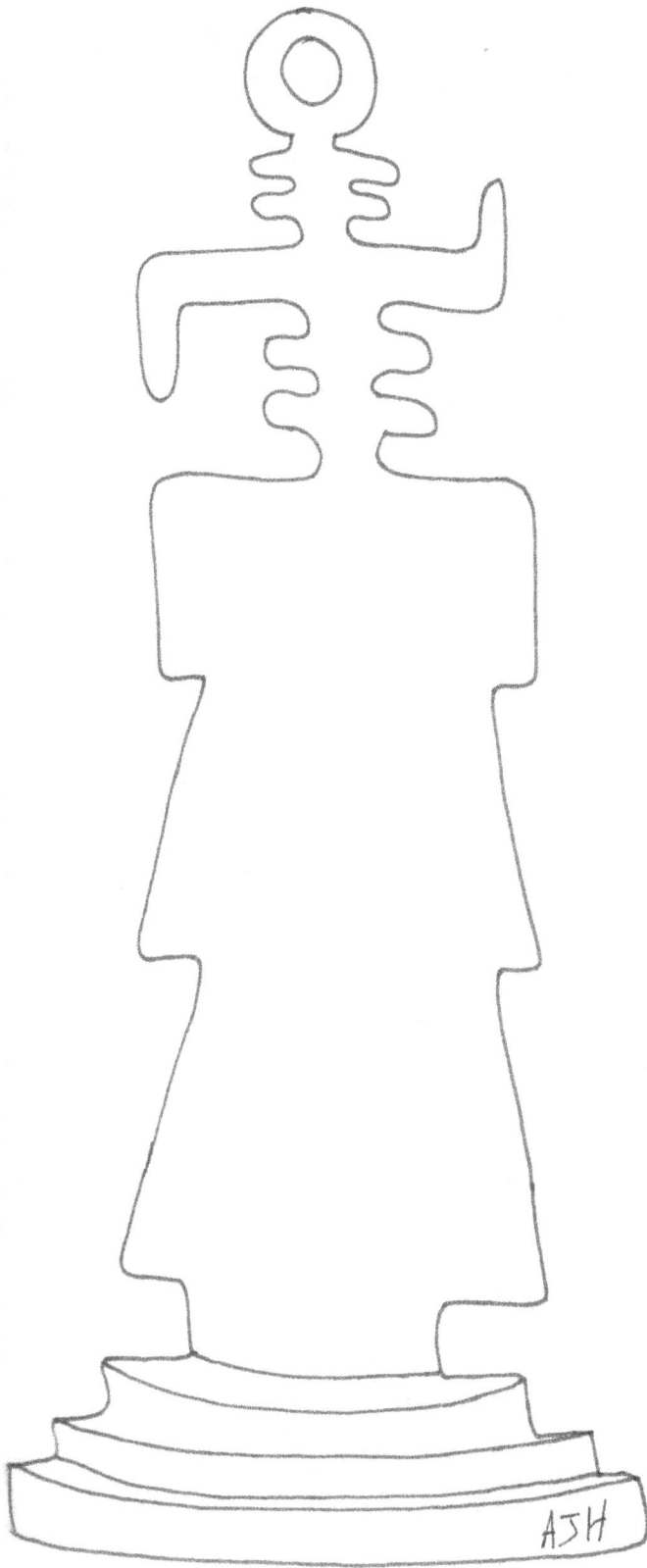

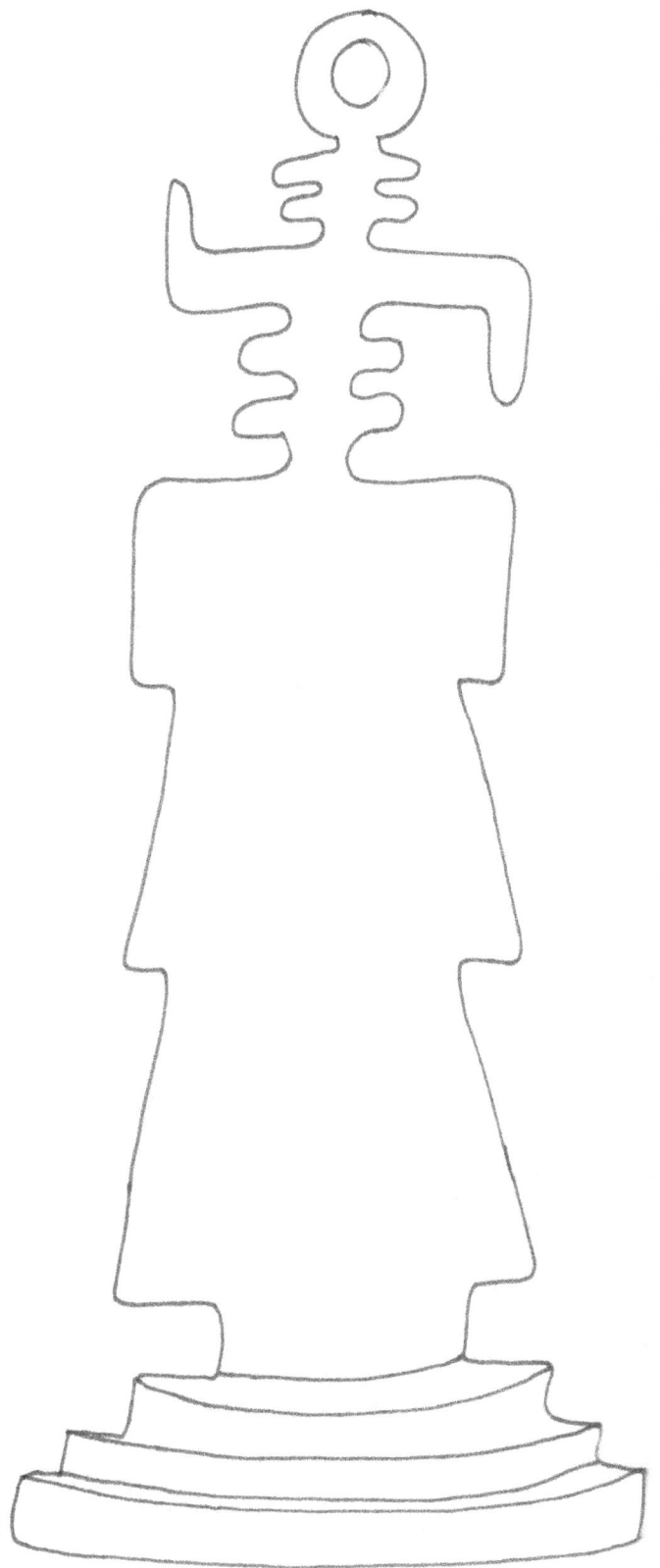

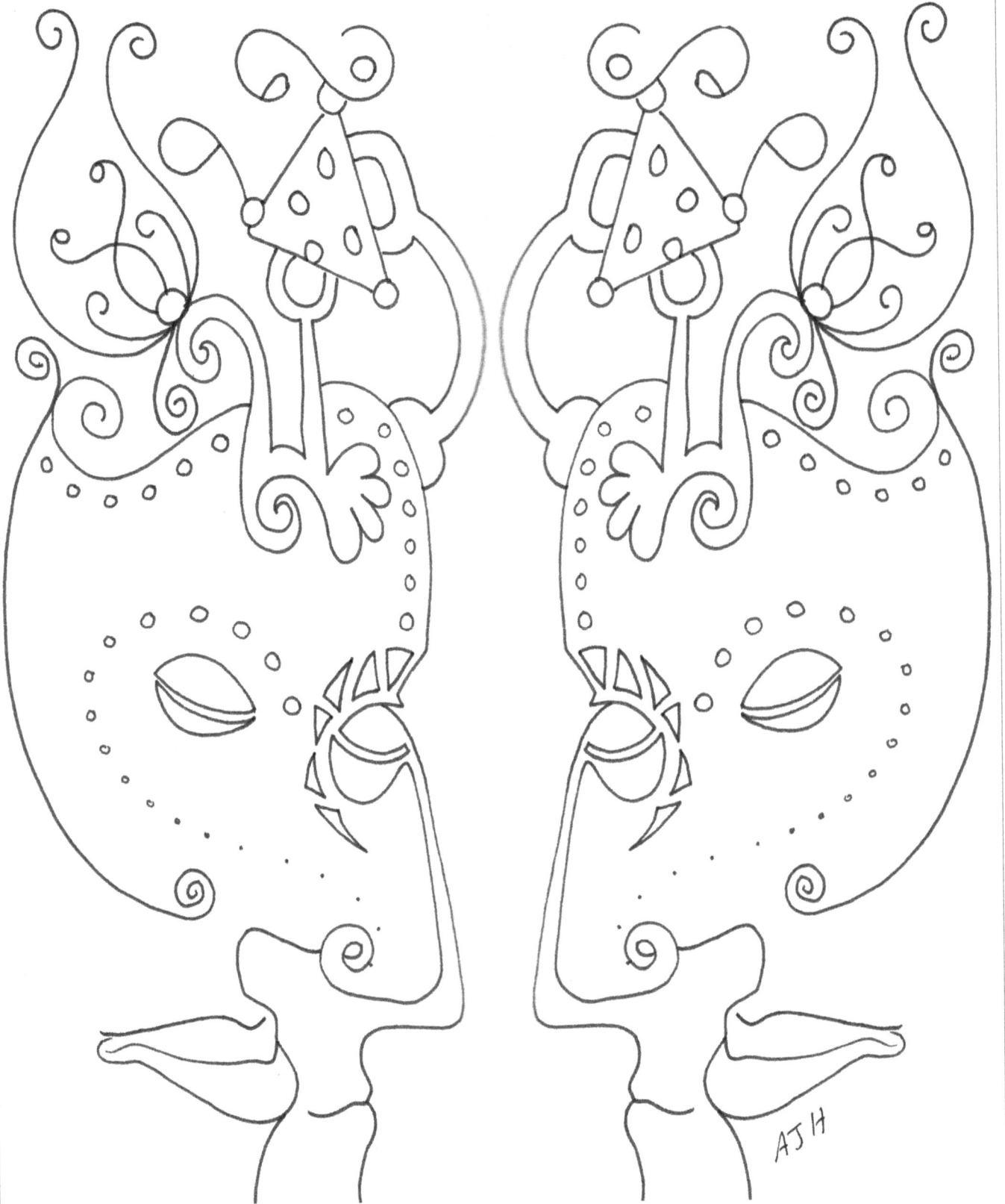

AJ H

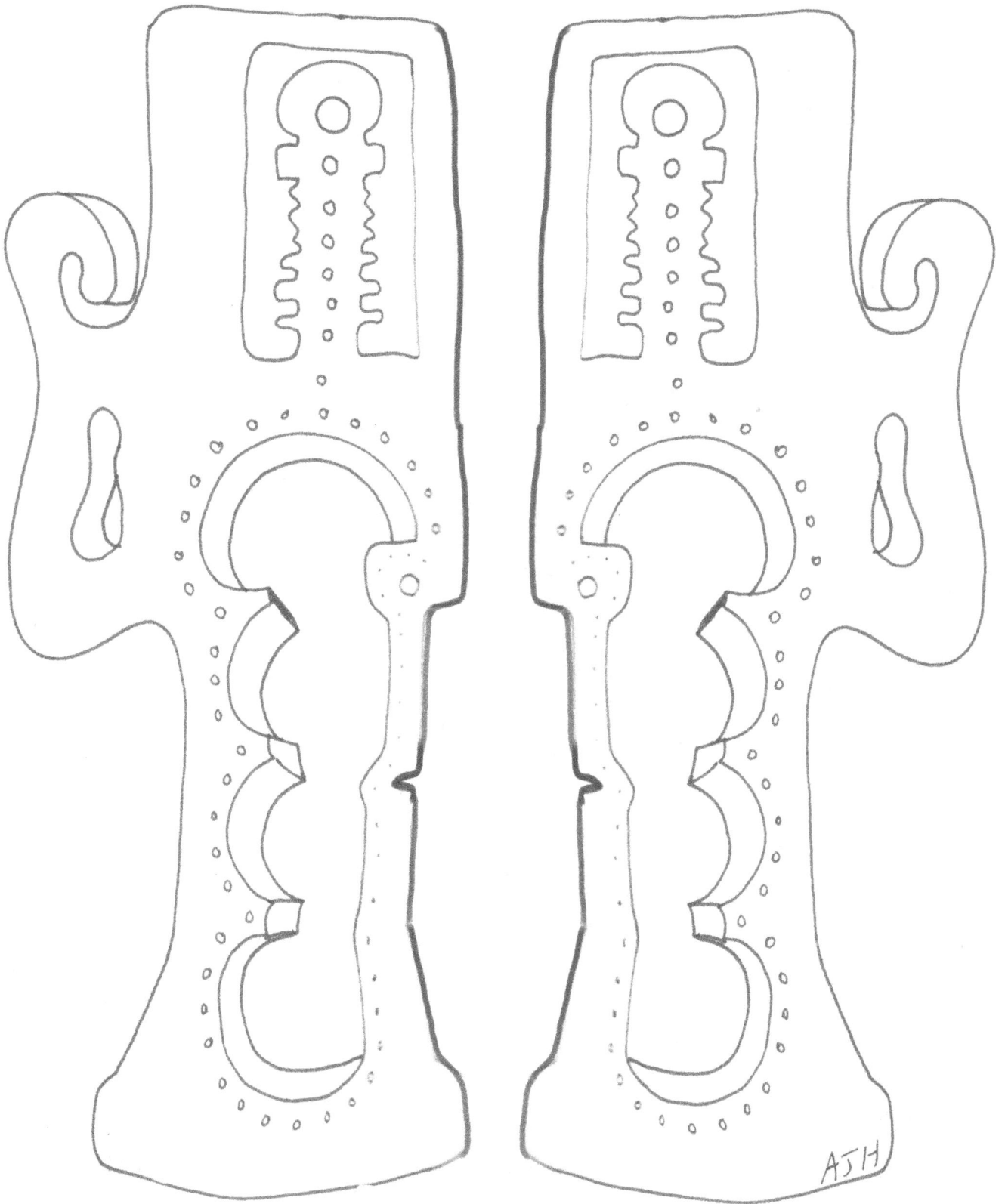

AJH

AJH   HƆA

AJH

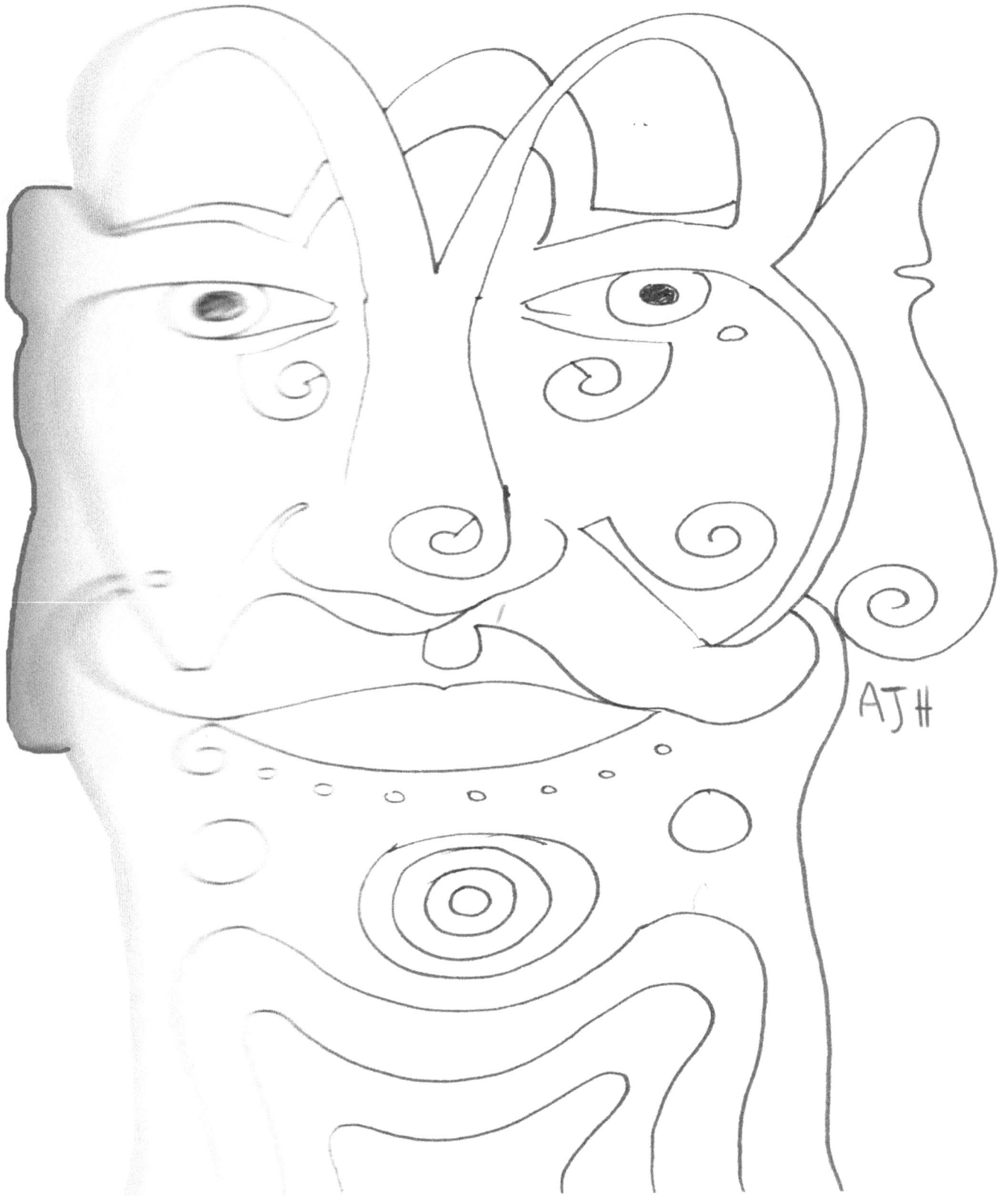

AJH

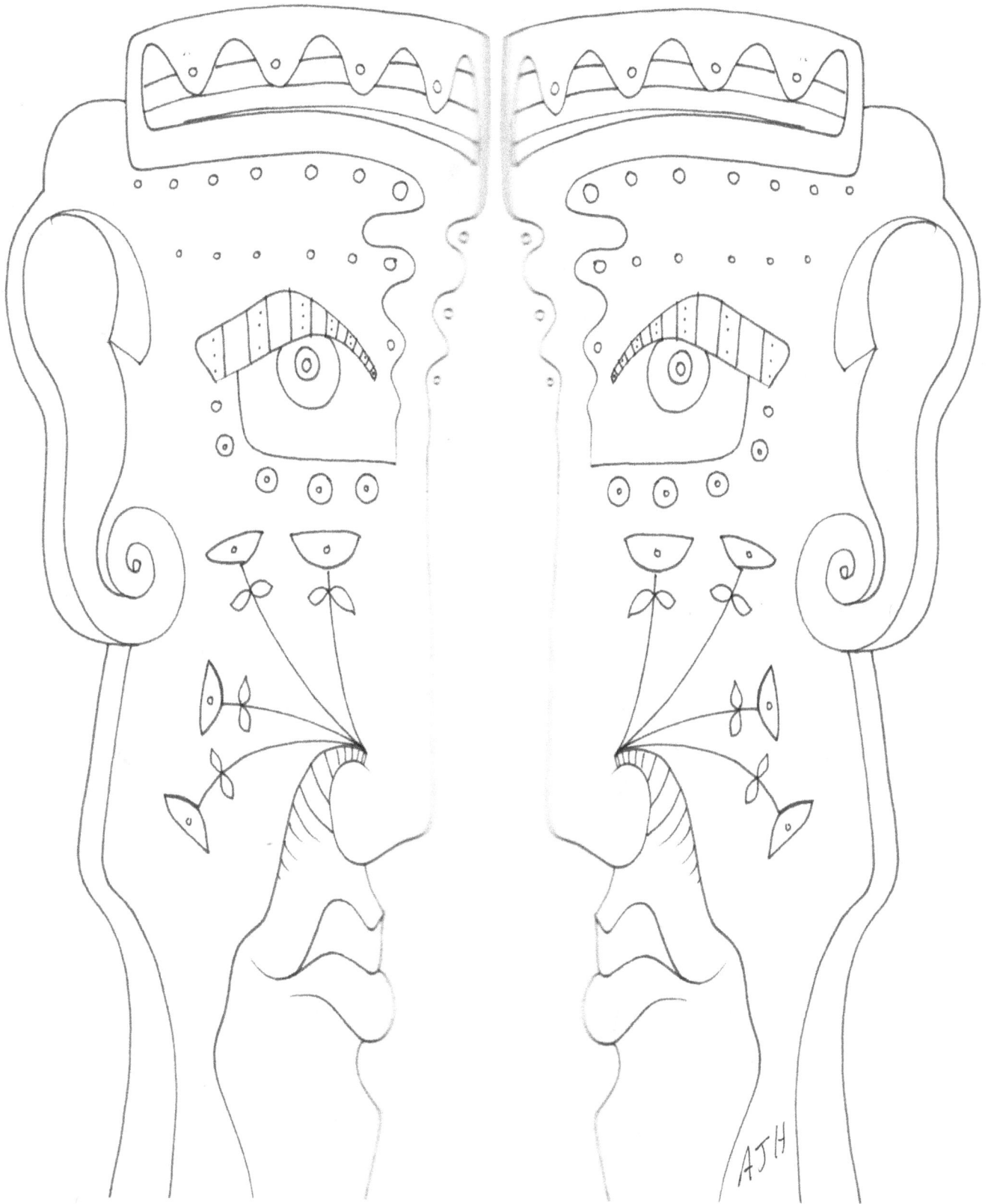

AJH

$$4^{10} + 8^9$$
$$10^{10} + 7^6$$
$$15^{10} + 8^7$$
$$\overline{X + Y = Z / 10\%}$$

HERE

AJH

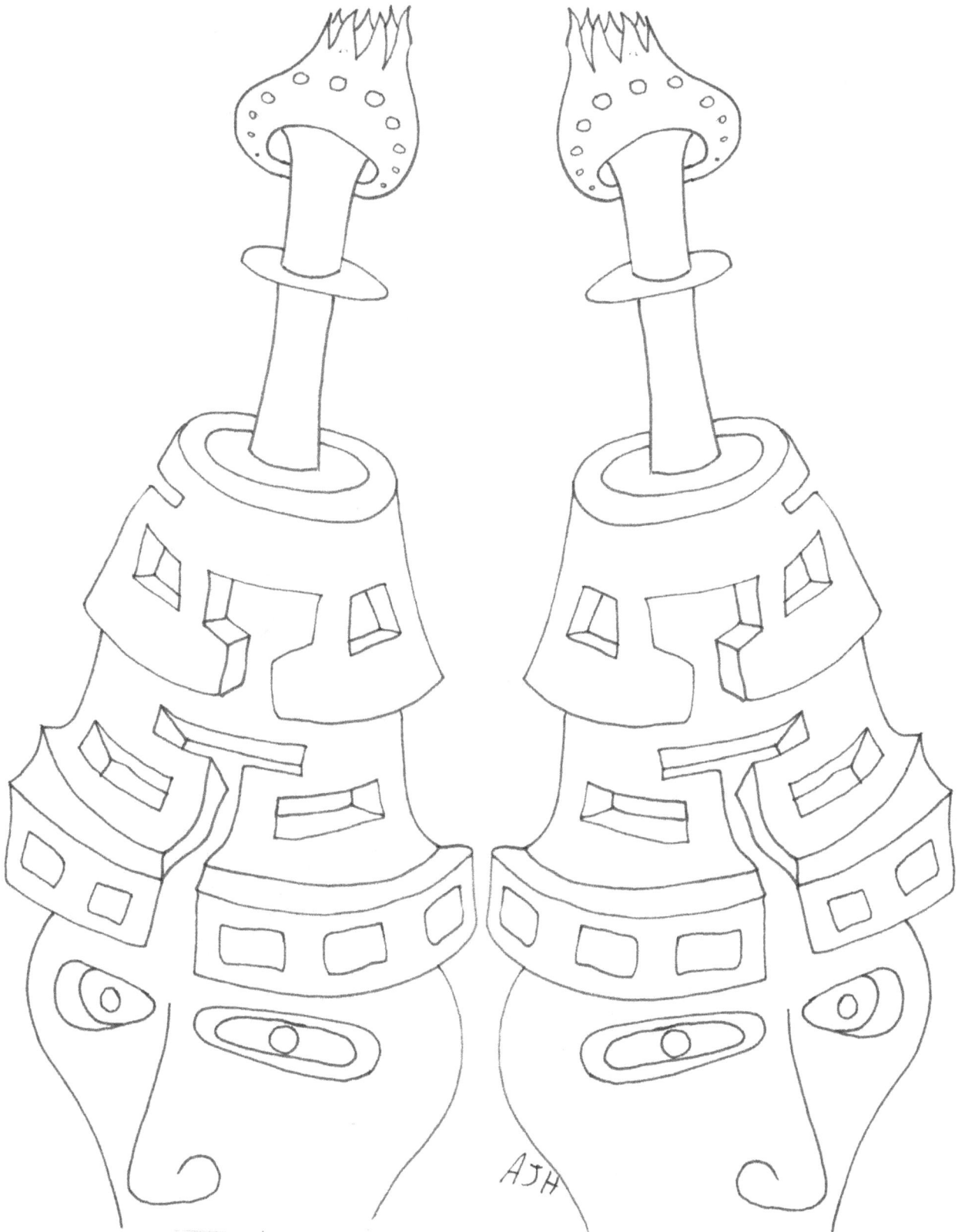

AJH

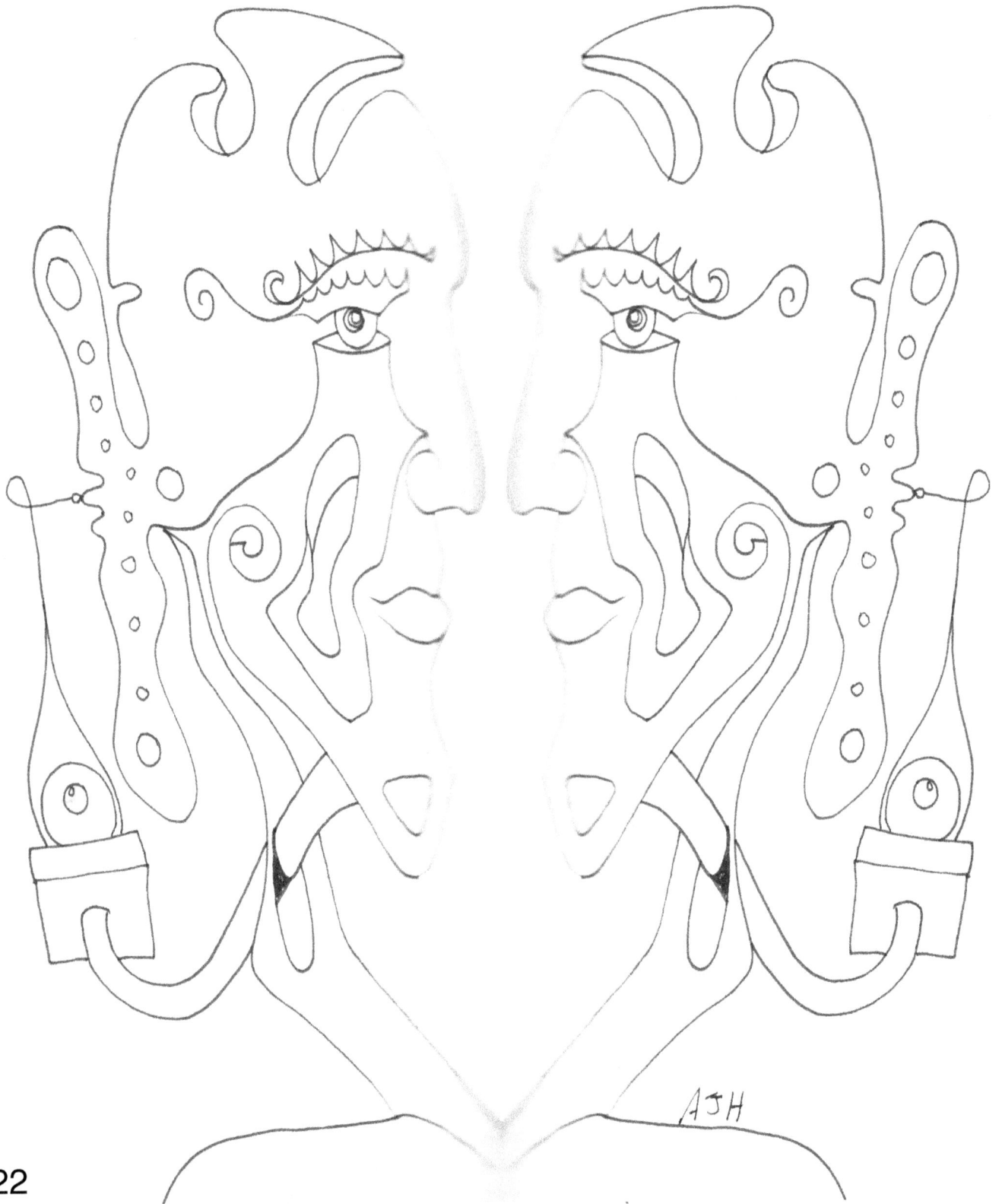

AJH

22

Modern Ned Publishing

Dedicated to bringing you great books of art. Books that are interactive, anti-stress and art therapy all rolled into one!

Our books are creative and imaginative, peaceful and interesting, different and spiritual, strange and wonderful, new and introspective, poetic and rhythmic, focused and serene. They are designed to bring you peace of mind while inspiring you to be creative with colours of your own choosing.

With our imagination, your creativity and a little colour our drawings will come alive. We hope you enjoy this book as well as other titles we have published.

"The Internal Gates"
"The Internal Highway"

To find more great art, visit our website
modernnedpublishing.ca

Please leave a review for this book, Thank you

Printed by CreateSpace, An Amazon.com Company

Sign up for our *newsletter*
signup@modernnedpublishing.ca

Get free images to downloads from up coming books.
Be the first to know when a new publication is ready for purchase.
See full colour images from the "The Internal Highway" series published by MNP
before they are shared on mass media.
Be the first to read the latest surreal poetry by AJH.
Enjoy some great photography and much more.

All images are the intellectual property
of the Artist
Alan John Hewitt
The Internal Portraits ISBN 978-0-9920060-5-1
Published by
Modern Ned Publishing
8 - 1010 Ellery Street
Esquimalt BC Canada
V9A-6Z8